Nothing can excel the extreme beauty of a well-constructed pergola; clothed in beautiful vines and flanked by borders of brilliant blooming Perennials.

California Gardens
of the Arts & Crafts Period

Eugene O. Murmann

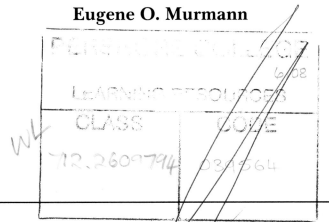
Take a tour of historic California garden design via this classic book. Released in 1914 the book offered yesterday's reader ways to plan and beautify the city lot, suburban grounds, and country estate. For today's historic home owner, there are 50 garden plans and 103 illustrations of actual gardens from photographs taken by the author. Of special interest are photos of outdoor furniture, lighting, and trellises. This book is a wealth of imagery and ideas about Arts & Crafts era sensibilities, Japanese gardens, and Mission-influenced landscape design.

4880 Lower Valley Road, Atglen, Pennsylvania 19310

Preface

There is little biographical information to be found on Eugene O. Murmann (1874-1962). He was born in Russia in 1874 and later settled in Glendale, California, according to "Artists in California, 1786-1940" by Edan Hughes. Besides being an artist and landscaper, he received for a patent for a can opener in 1922. However, his legacy for the Arts and Crafts Movement on the merits of this book is huge. He is credited with coining California garden style by the National Park Service, and his work helped establish direction for a wildly growing population of bungalows from the time of the book's release in 1914 through the 1930s.

This wonderful, Arts & Crafts Era volume comes back to life to serve as an aid to those endeavoring to restore historic authenticity to their neighborhoods.

Eugene O. Murmann's book was one of several influential guides to the homeowners across the nation who were experiencing a newfound urge to create in the blossoming environment of the bungalow. Many of these "kit" homes were being built in the growing suburban environment on the United States. Murmann helped direct the new homeowner's efforts to beautify their lots in ways harmonious with an aesthetic that celebrated the rustic, accessible spirit of the Arts & Crafts Era.

The author provides fifty beautiful plot plans and 103 photographs of actual gardens real photos are invaluable for anyone who wants to recreate the aesthetic of the California suburb circa early 1900s. The author endeavored to keep his text and illustrations straightforward and simple, making this book as useful today as it was almost 100 years ago.

Copyright © 2008 by Schiffer Publishing, Ltd.
Library of Congress Control Number: 2007938037

ISBN: 978-0-7643-2861-9
Printed in China

Schiffer Books are available at special discounts for bulk purchases for sales promotions or premiums. Special editions, including personalized covers, corporate imprints, and excerpts can be created in large quantities for special needs. For more information contact the publisher:

Published by Schiffer Publishing Ltd.
4880 Lower Valley Road
Atglen, PA 19310
Phone: (610) 593-1777; Fax: (610) 593-2002
E-mail: Info@schifferbooks.com

For the largest selection of fine reference books on this and related subjects, please visit our web site at **www.schifferbooks.com**
We are always looking for people to write books on new and related subjects. If you have an idea for a book please contact us at the above address.

This book may be purchased from the publisher.
Include $3.95 for shipping.
Please try your bookstore first.
You may write for a free catalog.

In Europe, Schiffer books are distributed by
Bushwood Books
6 Marksbury Ave.
Kew Gardens
Surrey TW9 4JF England
Phone: 44 (0) 20 8392-8585; Fax: 44 (0) 20 8392-9876
E-mail: info@bushwoodbooks.co.uk
Website: www.bushwoodbooks.co.uk
Free postage in the U.K., Europe; air mail at cost.

CONTENTS

Alpine Garden ....No. 21

Bog Gardens ....Included in Nos. 20, 33

Colonial Gardens ....Nos. 41, 42

Corner Lots ....Nos. 31, 32, 33, 34, 35, 39, 50

Dutch Bulb Garden...No. 15

Formal Gardens.................Nos. 9, 11, 15, 24, 28, 31, 35, 38, 40, 44, 45, 46, 48, 49, 50

Heath Garden ....No. 18 and included in No. 50

Iris Garden ....No. 37

Japanese Flat Garden (Hira-niwa)... No. 16

Japanese Hill Garden (Tsukiyama-niwa)......................................No. 17

Japanese Iris Garden..No. 39

Japanese Tea Garden (Cha-niwa)..No. 39

Landscape Gardens ....Nos. 29, 32, 43, 45, 47, 48, 49, 50

Natural Gardens ....Nos. 1, 3, 6, 10, 12, 13, 19, 29, 32, 34, 36

Old English Gardens...Nos. 22, 23

Old-Fashioned Garden ....No. 7

Perennial Borders ....Included in Nos. 10, 49, 50

Rock and Water Gardens...Nos. 20, 21, 33

Rose Gardens ....Nos. 4, 8, 14, 25, 26, 27, and included in Nos. 44, 50

Semi-formal Gardens ....Nos. 2, 5, 30, 43, 47

Special Color Schemes—Blue and silver gray in Nos. 36, 47, 50.
                Red and white in No. 50.
                Yellow and white in No. 50.
                Yellow and red in No. 50.
                Dark blue and autumn tints in No. 50.

INTRODUCTION

THE object of this book is to make it possible at small expense for any one to have a well-arranged, artistic garden. This book is brief —it is right to the point—it will help you wonderfully in the betterment and improvement of your property.

A great many people who have lawns or back yards suitable for gardens do not feel that they can afford the services of an expert landscape architect in addition to the cost of the planting material required to transform their surroundings into a place of beauty. With this book in hand this obstacle is overcome, and any one, even those who have never had any experience before in garden making, should be able to have just as perfect a garden as any expert gardener could produce.

Most people who start in to plan a garden lay it out without any reference whatever to the general effect, crowding into a small space of ground many kinds of plants, irrespective of their habit and suitability for the conditions—and the result is invariably very poor or a flat failure.

A well-thought-out garden design and arrangement with a general working plan to accompany it is the very last thing that most beginners think of. If they were equipped with such a plan and a planting list of well-selected plants suitable for their particular conditions and climate, if they would only give a thought to the harmony and finished appearance of their garden, if they had some sort of simple guide to show them exactly where to put each plant to get the best effect and display, the result would be an effective garden with harmonious color scheme and succession of bloom throughout the season.

California gardens are classed among the most beautiful in the world. Many of the best gardens in Southern California and, in fact, the whole state are remarkably unusual, not simply because palms and semi-tropical plant life thrive in California, *but because the general arrangement was taken into consideration and each tree and plant set in its proper place.*

CALIFORNIA GARDENS

In this book you will find illustrations that show the best of California's gardens and what can be done both in a large and small way. Do not get the idea that it is impossible for you to have a California garden in your climate, for it really can be done. Not that you can have palms, poinsettias, or other semi-tropical plants, but substitutes for these ornamentations which are every bit as effective, and in many cases, just as beautiful.

The plans shown in this book are mainly designed for California bungalows—unusual bungalow ideas which were published in my book, "Typical California Bungalows" (see last page), but which could be used for any type of house.

Every plan is different, and no matter how little or how great your requirements may be, you will find a plan in this book that is particularly adapted to your needs.

For the general re-arrangement of your entire garden, including both front and back, you will find many ideas in this book of great value and help.

PLANTING LISTS

The various planting lists for the plans included in this book that will be suitable for every different state or climatic condition would make a volume entirely too lengthy and technical. When you find the plan in this book that suits you, I will furnish you a planting list for it, with plants selected to suit the climatic conditions of your locality, together with a blue print of a working plan, drawn to a scale of 1/8 of an inch to the foot (the large ones, 1/16, 1/32 of an inch to the foot. This plan will be divided into squares by lines, which, when laying out your garden, should be drawn on the ground, giving you the exact space and location of every individual plant. From these lines all measures can be taken and edges of walks and drives, etc., can then be staked out according to the plan. The cost of such a planting list and blue print of plan is very reasonable, and ranges in price from $1 up, according to the size and elaborate nature of the garden. For prices see page 116.

GARDEN STYLES

In compiling this book the author has striven to give a collection of all the different types of gardens which are popular in this country and abroad. It will be readily seen that any of these particular gardens are adaptable to your local conditions with perhaps two or three plants substituted in place of ones that are grown in quarters where such gardens have originated.

WHY YOU SHOULD HAVE A GARDEN

Every one who owns a home, whether it is a large or small one, is greatly interested in the effect and general appearance of its surroundings. The average man points with pride to his hedge of tea roses or his clematis arbor. In a neighborhood of homes the grounds that are willfully neglected are invariably the ones that are least attractive — and the ones that are worth the least money.

A man is said to be judged by the company he keeps—a home should be known by the beauty of its surroundings. If artistic surroundings and gardens were very costly (as they are when a landscape gardener is required), it would be very logical for few homes to boast of these attractions, but since this simply-worded book, "California Gardens," has been placed on the market, the barrier has been entirely removed and any home may now have a garden of surprising beauty and color harmony.

Eugene O. Murmann

Post Office Box 998
Los Angeles, California

The following illustrations are actual photographs taken by the author and presented here as representative of typical California Gardens.

A sidewalk showing beautiful planting schemes on either side.

A tropical sidewalk producing a fine long vista.

11

A well-constructed porte-cochere of exceptional beauty.

A driveway shaded by a weeping willow and a pepper tree.

A beautiful porte-cochere with an effective planting scheme.

A driveway of unusual tropical beauty.

A Colonial home in a beautiful California setting.

A pretty little garden gate with an arched top.

A charming garden entrance. Note the beautiful *Cedrus Deodora pendula*.

A garden gate showing a simple and effective construction.

The charming lily pool on the terrace

The large sun-dial on the lawn is a unique feature.

Where picturesque and the classic meet.

A beautiful pergola and garden terrace.

17

Bird's-eye view of a beautiful California formal garden.

Cedars form a splendid background to the solemn row of Bay trees.

18

The formal fountain seen from the lower terrace.

Beautiful Cedars separate the formal garden from the landscape.

An effective grouping of Bay trees and Evergreens.

This garden is a fine illustration of excellent taste in gardening.

Beautiful Pansy beds give a special note of charm.

Cedars with drooping branches form a picture of striking beauty.

An Italian terraced garden of wonderful beauty.

Here is a delightful garden spot with a fine grouping of trees.

A fine spot with a magnificent distant view.

In this exquisite garden you will find a beauty at every turn.

23

A pergola is a beautiful addition to any garden.

A well-constructed pergola with an octagonal terminal.

A very successful treatment to terminate a pergola.

A garden enclosure with a pergola-like top.

Garden steps leading to the house under a beautiful rose-covered pergola.

A fine example of a pergola used in connection with garden steps.

Note the effect of the stately Hollyhocks planted near a pergola

Artistically treated pergolas form a highly decorative feature in any garden.

This pergola offers a charming resting place in beautiful surroundings.

An out-door living-room with the charm of seclusion well preserved.

A pergola of pleasing design and effective planting scheme.

A delightfully commodious spot for entertaining your friends.

29

Rose arches are a beautiful addition to any garden.

A garden fence covered with profusely blooming Roses.

There is nothing lovelier than a rose arch like this.

Rose arches make a beautiful driveway.

Beautiful borders of Larkspur with an effective background of trees.

Pale blue Delphiniums edged with the Dusty Miller give a striking effect.

Flower-bowers of great beauty margin the pathways.

Specimens of fine statuary add to the beauty of this garden.

A beautiful Italian villa in an exquisite setting.

New Zealand flax and Papyrus margin this lovely pond.

A pleasing composition of water and pergola.

This wonderfully pretty water garden is always a focal point of attraction.

Beautiful Agapanthus and Cineraria form the foreground of
this charming water garden.

An artificial pond showing a perfect natural treatment and careful planting.

Stately Lotus and dainty Water Lilies create a water garden like this.

The rustic bridge with an effective background of lovely Lotus.

Mass-planting of flowers creates a picture of striking beauty.

Colorado Blue Spruce and Cedars bring a special charm in the landscape.

The desert garden in the distance produces a tropical effect.

A beautiful garden shaded by a wonderful California live oak tree.

A landscape garden of exceptional beauty.

Nothing is more beautiful in a landscape than the Himalayan Cedar (*Cedrus Deodora*).

A well-made garden path and steps on a hillside.

Beautiful effect obtained by mass-planting of Petunias between the Cedars and Arancarias.

A most artistic treatment of a small piece of ground.

A typical California bungalow in an excellent setting.

A fine example for a miniature landscape garden.

Small hillocks and dwarf Evergreens make this landscape.

A rustic arch for hanging fern baskets forms the porch entrance.

A charming garden porch with an excellent planting scheme.

A very effective pergola-like covering for a garden pavilion.

A splendid example for a Japanese tea-house.

CALIFORNIA GARDENS

A charming Japanese tea-house in proper surroundings.

Garden steps leading to a path through the beautiful landscape garden.

CALIFORNIA GARDENS

A charming Japanese miniature landscape garden.

A California bungalow with an effective Japanese garden arrangement.

A well-arranged Japanese hill garden in a California yard.

This Japanese garden shows many attractive features.

Stone lanterns are a prominent feature in Japanese Gardens.

The adoption of Japanese style in a Los Angeles Garden.

Japanese three-legged stone lantern. "Snow Scene" type.

Japanese three-legged stone lantern. "Snow scene" type.

Japanese four-legged stone lantern. "Snow Scene" type.

Japanese three-legged stone lantern. "Snow Scene" type.

Japanese stone lantern. "Kasuga" type.

Japanese Bronze lantern.

Japanese Bronze lantern.

52

Japanese stone lantern.
"Snow Scene" type.

Japanese wood lantern.

Japanese stone lantern.
"Kasuga" type.

53

A driveway lined with Agaves and Cacti.

A bit of desert in a California garden.

A Cactus garden has a charm of its own.

A fine collection of Cacti, Agaves and Yucca.

A well-built rustic pergola has many attractive features.

A Cactus-lined path produces a tropical effect.

A rustic pergola running through the desert garden.

A well-constructed and artistic garden seat.

57

A fine example for a rustic circular seat.

A simple and attractive garden seat.

A well-built rustic seat for a Natural garden.

Seats like this are only for an informal garden.

CALIFORNIA GARDENS

A charming picture created by proper use of Evergreens.

Cypress trees are always effective when planted near a formal pond.

CALIFORNIA GARDENS

NO. 1. NATURAL GARDEN.

The charm of the garden is not the monopoly of the rich. It is not secured merely by the expenditure of money; it comes really from the exercise of good taste and correct judgment in using the natural beauties to the greatest advantage. A garden can easily lose its charm and become too artificial if made too elaborate and have too little of the touch of Nature to inspire the proper sentiment. So it is evident that the ideal garden, which has all the charms of Nature and completely fulfills its purpose as a resting place in pleasant surroundings is within the reach of men of moderate means. There are many back yards in a great metropolis or a small town which are used as assembling places for clothes poles, ash cans, and similar things. Such an unsightly "back-yard" can easily be converted into a charming garden without great expenses. How this can be accomplished without any waste of space on a 25-foot lot, a size common in many suburban towns, is shown in this plan. In the back-yard we have a small piece of ground set apart for vegetable beds and the shed. A hardy perennial border runs along the south side of the garden and a winding path in front of it leads to the vegetable garden and the little pavilion "A". The latter is almost completely surrounded by beautiful flowering shrubberies and forms a screen for the vegetable garden beyond. Choice shrubs are planted along the north side of the garden and at the back of the bungalow, to hide the kitchen entrance. The tiny open space of lawn in the center has a few specimens of herbaceous plants. For details about the planting list see pages 8 and 116.

PLAN NO. 1
Size of Lot 25'x125'

CALIFORNIA GARDENS

NO. 2. SEMI-FORMAL GARDEN.

This plan gives a good idea of the suitability of the semi-formal style to small plots. It shows a beautiful rose arbor in the middle of the extreme end of the garden with shrubs planted in front, leaving openings between to allow a view of the entire garden on all sides. The tiny grass plot in the center of the garden has a row of standard roses along its edge and a round bed of brilliantly flowering annuals at its near end. In the remotest part of the lot, completely hidden by the rose arbor and shrubbery, is the shed and the small vegetable garden. The front is open to the street and has a flower bed near the porch. Flower borders form the boundary on either side of the bungalow. For details about the planting list see pages 8 and 116.

The plants and shrubs used in the garden are as important factors in the making of a garden as the plan itself. A good design may be entirely spoiled by incongruous planting. A knowledge of colors, habit and season of plants is needed in order to use them rightly and with the most pleasing effects. It is necessary to bear in mind the character and habit of each and every species and use it only in the position for which it is best adapted by nature. A mistake is often made in growing plants and shrubs in positions contrary to their natural habitat. The number of flowering shrubs and herbaceous plants is very great, and as they are all more or less beautiful, it is easy to make a selection adapted to the local conditions and at the same time produce the most beautiful results.

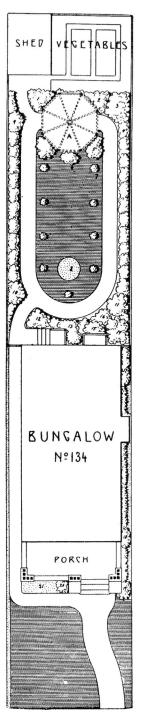

PLAN NO. 2
Size of Lot 25'x135'

CALIFORNIA GARDENS

NO. 3. NATURAL GARDEN.

Be it ever so humble, there is no place like a garden, nothing that will give more satisfaction and pleasure than the cultivation of flowers. Even the smallest plot is large enough for a garden, and its simple and tasteful arrangement together with proper care will often produce more charming results than many a pretentious one. A remarkably beautiful example of a small garden treated in a simple and informal way is shown in this plan. Its main feature in the background forms the octagonal pavilion—built of rustic material—which presents a pleasant place for out-door meals and recreation. Many varieties of beautiful flowering shrubs are planted in irregular groups along the fence, forming a hedge. A path of stepping-stones running along the shrubbery line to the left leads to the pavilion and to the small shed in the back yard. There are rockeries in front of the pavilion and near the path which leads to the kitchen entrance. Flowers are scattered on the lawn in little colonies and allowed to grow in a natural way. The front yard is open to the street and the lawn is continuous with those of the adjoining properties. Beautiful flowers are planted in the border along the south side of the bungalow and in front of the porch. A few choice shrubs arranged in groups on either side of the porch complete the planting scheme in the front. A small space in the back yard is reserved for vegetable beds. For the details about planting list see pages 8 and 116.

PLAN NO. 3
Size of Lot 35'x135'

63

NO. 4. ROSE GARDEN.

No flower better deserves a garden to itself than the ever-beloved and glorious rose. It is a place where the real lover of flowers can pay all his attention to the cultivation of the "Queen of Flowers." A very conveniently arranged rose garden for a narrow lot is shown in this plan. The pergola in the far end of the garden completely covered with profusely blooming roses, forms the central motive. In front of it is a U-shaped rose bed, which together with the two angular ones, encloses an open space of turf with a sun-dial in the center. Opposite the pergola at the near end of the garden is a beautiful rose arch. Grass paths, flanked by rose borders, lead to the small kitchen garden and the shed in the rear of the lot. It is well screened from the rose garden and contains a few beds for vegetables. An evergreen hedge completely encircling the place, gives the grounds a delightful feeling of seclusion. On the lawn in front of the charming bungalow are two beautiful shade-trees with groups of choice flowering shrubs near the porch. Behind the bungalow there are beautiful shrubs, cleverly arranged to hide the unsightly kitchen entrance. A garden like this is inexpensive to plant and could be laid out in any part of the country. The great number of the different varieties of roses permits the selection of numerous species and garden forms adapted to almost every requirement. For details about the planting list, see pages 8 and 116.

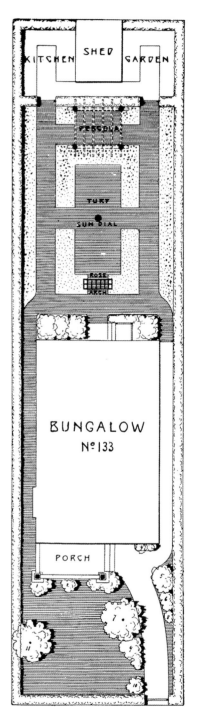

PLAN NO. 4
Size of Lot 35'x135'

CALIFORNIA GARDENS

NO. 5—SEMI-FORMAL GARDEN

An exceptionally clever design for a small garden on a narrow lot is shown in this plan. It is composed of two parts, separated from each other by an octagonal rose arbor, which forms the central motive in the garden. Overgrown by profusely blooming roses and flanked on the sides by beautiful shrubs this arbor offers a pleasant retreat in quiet surroundings with charming vistas in every direction. The lawn in the front section has a row of standard roses planted along the edge and a couple of choice shrubs placed in the two corners. Masses of shrubbery back of the bungalow hide the kitchen entrance entirely, and beautiful herbaceous borders run along the fence on either side of the garden. All the plants are so selected that they give a continuous bloom throughout the season. The crescent-shaped lawn in the rear section of the garden has four dwarf evergreens. A group of shrubbery planted in front of the entrance to the back yard screens it from the garden side. A hedge of various shrubs encloses this part of the garden, forming a screen to hide the shed and the small vegetable garden (in the back yard). In each upper corner, surrounded by shrubbery, is a garden seat, painted to match the color of the trim of the dwelling. The planting in the front yard is simple and consists of choice shrubs, arranged in groups on either side of the porch, and herbaceous plants along the south side of the bungalow. There are two dwarf evergreens planted on either side of the approach. The north side being provided with ferns and other shade-loving plants. For details about the planting list, see pages 8 and 116.

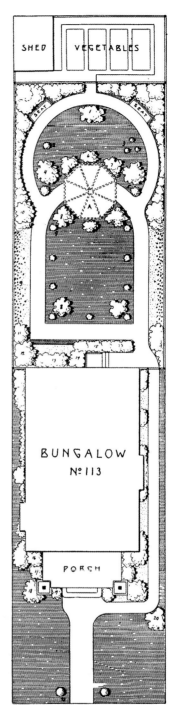

PLAN NO. 5
Size of Lot 35'x150'

CALIFORNIA GARDENS

NO. 6—NATURAL GARDEN

Whether large or small, a garden should be simple in its design. Simplicity is the result of a well-ordered plan by which the garden becomes not merely a collection of trees, shrubs and flowers, but a coherent entity, charming as a whole as well as in its details. Simplicity is the keynote in this little plan. A wide path leads from the kitchen entrance to the shed and small vegetable garden in the remotest part of the lot. A narrow path branches to the right, and after passing along the shrubbery line, joins the first one again, leaving a kidney-shaped lawn in the center. Beautiful flowering shrubs enclose the place on all sides and give it a reasonable amount of privacy. The planting on the lawn consists of a few groups of choice shrubs and herbaceous plants properly arranged. A suitable place for flowers is provided in the corner near the bungalow. The plan shows a small oval bed in an open space of lawn, but a still better effect could be obtained by utilizing the entire space for hardy perennials. In the right-hand corner, at the far end of the garden, is a seat surrounded by shrubbery. A flower bed runs along the south side of the bungalow and across in front of the porch. A hedge of low shrubs forms the boundary on either side of the bungalow. The front is open to the street, the lawn being continuous with those of the adjoining properties. A few shrubs, grouped near the porch and on either side of the walk, complete the planting. The vegetable garden contains a few vegetable beds and is large enough to supply fresh vegetables for a small family. For details about the planting list, see pages 8 and 116.

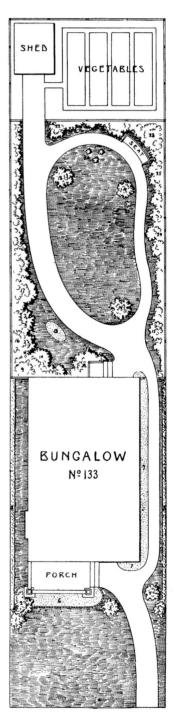

PLAN NO. 6
Size of Lot 35'x150'

NO. 7—OLD-FASHIONED GARDEN

The old-fashioned gardens were modest, planned on the simple idea of using plants that grew easily and naturally with perhaps the slightest effort, and certainly with utmost flowering. The materials which the old-time gardeners used were few and unimportant. They made borders of ready growing annuals; they planted shrubs which were easy to cultivate and were content to transform the homely back yard into a bower of bloom and foliage. This plan shows a small garden laid out on the lines of the old-fashioned gardens, simple in design, abundant in flowering shrubs and hardy plants. It is composed of four rectangular beds bordered with box and planted with brilliant flowering plants and choice shrubbery. At the far end of the garden is a little arbor almost hidden in flowers and masses of shrubbery. A delightful place where one can rest in quiet seclusion and for a while forget cares and find renewed energies. At the near end of the axial path, directly opposite the pavilion, is a garden seat flanked on either side by beautiful shrubbery. An arched rose bower near the intersection of the central path adds much to the beauty of the garden. A border of hardy perennials and shrubbery encloses the garden on all sides, giving it the delightful feeling of seclusion. The front lawn is planted with choice flowers and shrubbery groups near the porch and along the boundary. For details about the planting list, see pages 8 and 116.

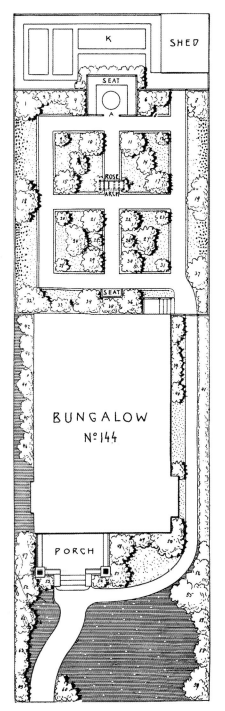

PLAN NO. 7
Size of Lot 40'x135'

NO. 8—ROSE GARDEN

This plan represents an ideal rose garden, laid out in typical formal style, with paths arranged in a geometrical design. Its central feature is the arbor, which is entirely covered by climbing masses of beautiful roses, and forms a fragrant and pleasant retreat on hot summer days. The central path passes through beautiful rose arches and is terminated by a semi-circular rose arbor. A dense hedge encloses the garden on all sides and gives it the charm of seclusion. A garden seat, painted to match the trim of the building, is placed in the shrubbery back of the bungalow and a view obtained from there, looking through the arches when completely covered by profusely blooming roses, is lovely beyond description. The walks are either of gravel or turf, the latter ones being preferable. A small piece of ground is set apart in the back yard for vegetables and the shed. Ferns and various plants which thrive in the shade are planted on the north side of the bungalow, the south side being adorned with groups of herbaceous plants and beautiful flowering shrubs. The planting in front of the bungalow is simple and attractive. It is composed mostly of choice flowering shrubs, arranged in groups, and of herbaceous plants in front of the porch. The lawn is continuous with those of the neighboring gardens. A thin hedge forms the boundary on the north side. For details about the planting list, see pages 8 and 116.

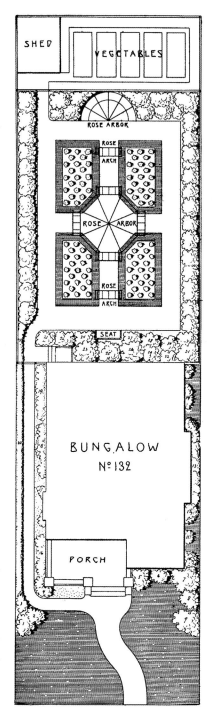

PLAN NO. 8
Size of Lot 40′x145′

NO. 9—FORMAL GARDEN

Here is a splendid little plan for a formal garden on a 40-foot lot. It is a great rectangle and comparatively simple in design — four lawns placed around a central circle, each lawn having a round central bed and being surrounded with wide borders edged with box. All these beds are beautifully planted with shrubs and brilliantly flowering herbaceous plants. In the middle of the central circle is a sun-dial surrounded by a flower bed. The central motive at the far end of the garden is an octagonal arbor combined with a pergola, which separates the humble vegetable garden from its brilliant neighbor. Groups of beautiful flowering shrubs are planted along the back of the bungalow, hiding the kitchen entrance. A garden seat, painted to match the trim of the building, is placed at the near end of the central path, directly opposite the arbor, a point from where pleasant vistas are obtained. The garden is screened and protected on both sides by means of shrubberies. Flower borders run along the south side of the bungalow and in front of the porch. On the sides the lot is enclosed by a hedge, the straight lines of which are relieved by a few flowering shrubs. The small vegetable garden in the back yard contains four fruit trees —vegetable bed and the shed. Omitting the back yard, this plan could be used on a 135-foot lot. The lawn in front of the bungalow is open to the street. For details about the planting list, see pages 8 and 116.

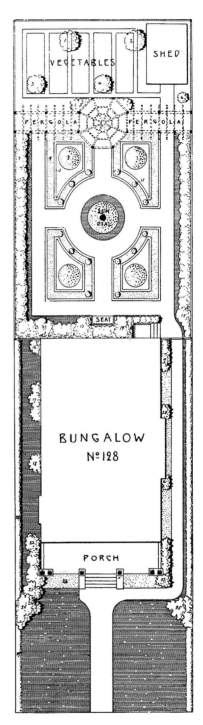

PLAN NO. 9
Size of Lot 40'x150'

NO. 10—NATURAL GARDEN

The picturesqueness of a naturalistic treatment in the garden is well displayed in this plan. It shows a place enclosed on all sides by irregular groupings of various shrubs, giving it that charm of privacy which makes it the most peasant of out-of door rooms. Brilliant borders of hardy perennials so selected that, throughout the season, there will be a constant succession of bloom, are planted along the shrubbery hedges. Gravel walks winding along these borders lead to the pergola in the extreme end of the garden, where on hot summer days a cool retreat is found. (To give the place a more natural appearance, these walks could be substituted by paths of stepping stones.) On the lawn are a few choice evergreens and shrubs, which are planted near the pergola and along the path, where they can display their beauty to the greatest advantage, and to the effect of the garden as a whole. A rustic garden seat is placed in the shrubbery near the building and gives a charming view in every direction. There is a garage and a small vegetable garden in the back yard with a separate entrance from the alley. Flower borders run along the south side of the bungalow and in front of the cozy porch. The front lawn is open to the street with a few evergreens and shrubs planted in groups, as indicated in the plan. For details about the planting list, see pages 8 and 116.

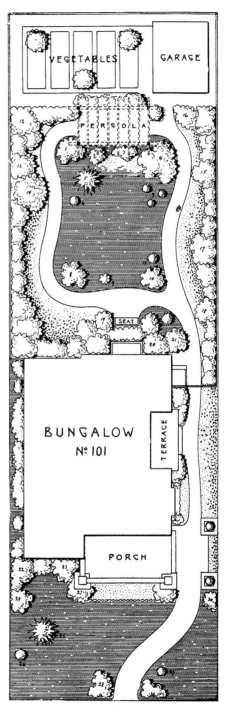

PLAN NO. 10
Size of Lot 45'x145'

NO. 11. FORMAL GARDEN

This plan shows quite an unusual design and a garden of strongly marked individuality. The commanding feature of it is the pergola, which stretches back from the circular path, bounded on the sides by open spaces of lawn and at the far end by another pergola. The latter is enclosed on three sides by various flowering shrubs, the front being planted with climbing roses with openings to give a glimpse of the lawn and the beautiful herbaceous borders, along the boundary line. This beautiful pergola furnished with easy chairs and tea table and so surrounded by shrubs that the charm of seclusion is well preserved, makes a delightful place to rest. The front part of the garden has a round lily pond, edged with various plants, which grow on the waterside. Choice flowering shrubs are planted back of the bungalow, along the side of the garage and the fence opposite. A garden seat is placed in the shrubbery near the building, opposite the pergola entrance, allowing a splendid vista of the entire scenery. The little vegetable garden is well screened from the garden side and can be reached either from the rear pergola or the entrance between the garage and the fence. Along the drive are shrubs and herbaceous plants, which form the boundary. The front lawn is open on to the street, and has a few choice shrubs near the building. For details about the planting list, see pages 8 and 116.

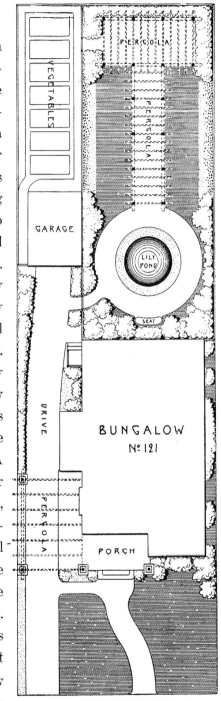

PLAN NO. 11
Size of Lot 45'x150'

NO. 12. NATURAL GARDEN

The special elements of beauty in this little garden are simplicity of line and richness in detail of planting. Two paths lead by graceful curves to a little pavilion, almost entirely hidden in masses of beautiful flowering shrubbery. Groups of shrubs are planted along the back of the bungalow, hiding the kitchen entrance. The garage, with the little vegetable garden back of it, is screened by irregular groups of choice shrubbery. A mixed herbaceous border runs along the boundary line opposite the garage. On the lawn are a few shrubs and evergreens planted in attractive groups in front of the pavilion and near the garden entrance. The front is open to the street, the lawn being continuous with those of the neighboring gardens. The planting on the lawn is simple and attractive, consisting of a couple of low evergreens on either side of the walk, a specimen conifer on the lawn near the boundary and a few selected flowering shrubs in front of the bungalow. The terrace on the side of the dwelling is flanked by herbaceous plants and a hardy flower border runs along the drive, forming the boundary line. For details about the planting list, see pages 8 and 116.

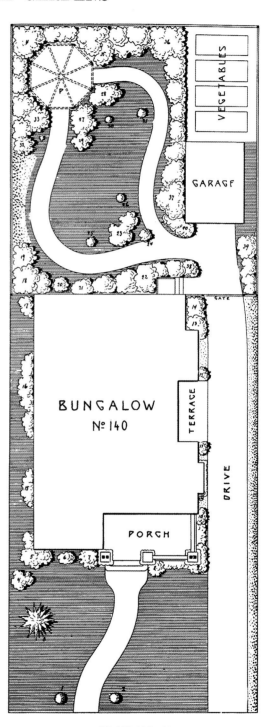

PLAN NO. 12
Size of Lot 50'x135'

NO. 13. NATURAL GARDEN

It is difficult to characterize the beauties of so lovely a place as this little natural garden. The entire place is an unbroken surface of lawn, bordered on all sides by irregular groups of flowering shrubs, with a few selected shrubs planted here and there. The pergola in the extreme end of the garden is a pleasant retreat on hot summer days and the little lily pond before it brings the charm of water into the garden and provides an ideal home for beautiful pond lilies and many aquatic plants. A rustic garden seat, surrounded by shrubs, is placed near the bungalow, directly opposite the pond, and a winding path of stepping stones leads from it to the pergola and the entrance gate. Spring flowers are scattered about in the turf in drifts and little colonies, imitating Nature's picture as near as possible. Back of the garage is the little kitchen garden, well hidden from the adjoining garden by means of shrubbery. The sides of the lot are enclosed by an evergreen hedge, and a suitable place for flowers is provided in the border along the drive, and on both sides of the pergola-covered terrace. For details about the planting list, see pages 8 and 116.

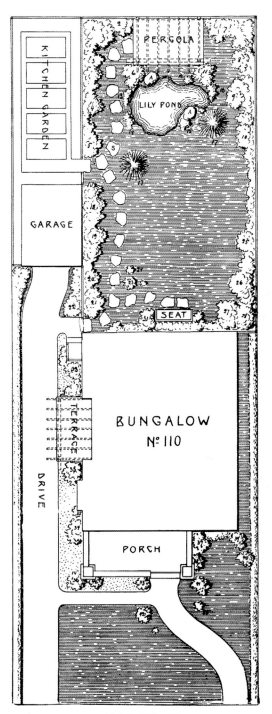

PLAN NO. 13
Size of Lot 50'x135'

NO. 14. ROSE GARDEN

Nothing in nature is more beautiful than roses. Their beauty of form, their glorious colors, and their fragrance endear them to all, and a garden devoted entirely to the cultivation of these exquisite flowers will be a source of unending pleasure. This plan shows a beautiful rose garden in which a series of rose arches, connected by side pieces, form a semi-circle enclosing the garden on three sides. Back of this semi-circle and forming part of it are two rose arbors. The background is screened with beautiful shrubbery and hides the little vegetable garden beyond. In the middle of the garden is a round bed on which stands a sun-dial. Back of the bungalow are groups of shrubbery with a garden seat in the center. Opposite the seat is a short walk, which leads through a rose arch to the circular path bordered by standard roses. The front is open to the street, the lawn being continuous with the neighboring gardens. Groups of choice flowering shrubs are planted around the porch and along the path leading to the back garden. On either side of the bungalow the lot is enclosed by an evergreen hedge and a flower border runs along the south side of the dwelling. For details about the planting list, see pages 8 and 116.

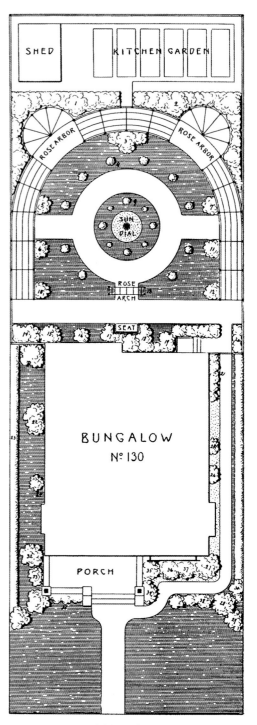

PLAN NO. 14
Size of Lot 50'x145'

NO. 15. DUTCH BULB GARDEN

Spring flowering bulbs are included among the plants specialized in garden making. The Dutch Bulb Garden is particularly welcome, because it displays its gorgeous bloom in a season, when the desire for flowers is greatest. The effect of these splendid flowers is superb, and nothing could excel the extreme beauty of the picture presented by their radiance, contrasted with the dark blue hue of the brick walks and the luxuriant green of the hedge, that forms the boundary of such a garden.

A Dutch Bulb Garden should be severely formal, and the accompanying plan shows a very convenient arrangement of paths and beds. In the middle of the central bed is a sun-dial, four beds placed around a circular path and surrounded by four corner beds alternated with four circular ones. In the middle of the outer border near the house is placed a garden seat, painted white. The walks are of blue brick. A Dutch Bulb Garden is easiest of all to care for, as the majority of the bulbs are permanent and increase in beauty from year to year. The main point is to obtain and plant the best kinds, it is only these that give the best display. For details about the planting list, see pages 8 and 116.

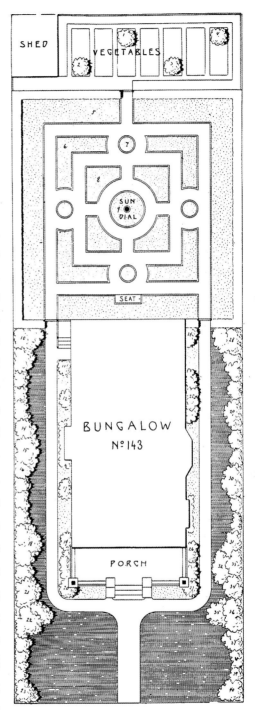

PLAN NO. 15
Size of Lot 50'x145'

NO. 16. JAPANESE FLAT GARDEN (Hira-niva)

The style of garden composition practiced in Japan is the natural style. Their landscape gardens are simple representations of natural views in miniature. A characteristic of Japanese gardening is the importance attached to the use of natural stones, rocks and boulders. The principal rocks and stones having names, which refer to their position in the landscape or represent the names of Buddhist deities. The type of garden shown in this plan is the "Hira-Niva," or flat garden. In the foreground is a well "W," made of roughly hewn stone with an overhanging dwarf pine. Adjoining the veranda is a group formed by a water basin "B," a stone lantern "L," and a screen with a trained pine tree behind it. The group in the middle is composed of a stone pagoda "P," pine tree, some low shrubs ("Marumono," see page 43), and "Guardian" stone No. 1. In the background on the west side of the garden is a stone lantern "L," a pair of stones No. 5 with a tree behind them. On the east side, near the entrance gate to the vegetable garden, is another group of stones No. 3, and a stone lantern "L." A path of stepping stones leads from the veranda to the garden gates, branching towards the well on one side and towards the water basin on the other. The plain open portions are usually spread with sand or a firm surface of beaten earth. Turf has been introduced only recently in imitation of foreign methods. For details about the planting list, see pages 8 and 116.

PLAN NO. 16
Size of Lot 50'x145'

CALIFORNIA GARDENS

NO. 17. JAPANESE HILL GARDEN
(Tsukiyama-niva)

An ideal Japanese landscape must contain a combination of mountains and water scenery. The Hill Garden (Tsukiyama-niva) style is the model of a most complete Japanese garden. The present plan shows such a garden with little hillocks, "ABCD," representing mountains. "B" is placed in the remotest part of the garden and is meant to represent a distant peak, visible over the sides of hills "A" and "C," which form the central feature of the nearer distance. A cascade and rocks mark the division between the two. "D" is a low, rounded hill in the foreground, covered with detail in the form of stones and shrubs, without any characteristics of a large or distant mountain. There are many important rocks or stones in the garden, of which No. 1, the "Guardian Stone," occupies the most central position in the background; it represents the presiding genius of the garden, and together with No. 3, the "Worshipping Stone," must be introduced into all Japanese gardens. The little lake fed by a waterfall is an almost indispensable feature of Japanese gardens, and even in localities where no natural supply can be obtained, the water scenery is expressed by a sunken stretch of bare beaten earth or well-raked sand (as in plan No. 16), with isolated stones scattered here and there to indicate islands. A bridge, two ornamental stone lanterns, "L," the water basin "W," a number of selected trees and shrubs complete the landscape. For details about the planting list, see pages 8 and 116.

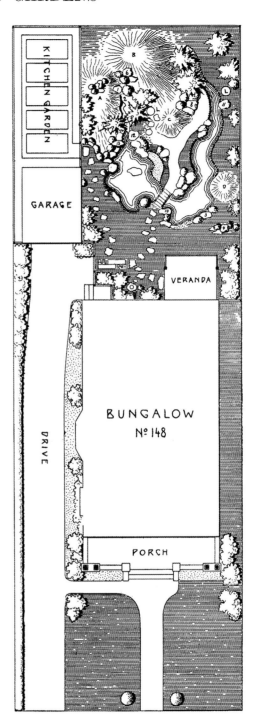

PLAN NO. 17

Size of Lot 50'x145'

77

CALIFORNIA GARDENS

NO. 18—HEATH GARDEN

The great beauty of the heath (Erica) can only be judged by those who have seen it growing naturally on mountains and moors, where it is among the most beautiful of plants in the effect of broad masses. Such picturesque effects, of course, can be shown only in large gardens, but to enjoy their beauty a small one is large enough to grow a few hardy heaths on a small scale. The heaths are easy to cultivate and when once established, they need very little attention. There are many charming kinds which are hardy in the northern and eastern states, the tender ones, however, may be grown in the southern and southwestern states. This plan shows a little heath garden 50 x 65. The extreme end of the garden is composed of coniferous trees, which form a splendid background. The sides are planted with shrubs, which group harmoniously with the heath and at the same time form a screen to hide some feature which is out of harmony. The ground is gently undulating and slopes slightly towards the central path, thus giving a naturally broken surface, which will prevent the possibility of monotony. The heath is planted in groups of irregular shape with no distinct dividing line between the different species. For details about the planting list, see pages 8 and 116.

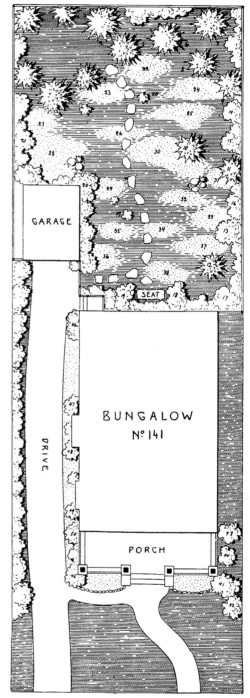

PLAN NO. 18
Size of Lot 50'x150'

NO. 19—NATURAL GARDEN

This plan represents a little city garden on a 50 x 150 lot. The planting is simple and attractive. It is composed of a few trees and many choice flowering shrubs, planted along the boundary, screening and protecting the garden on all sides and leaving in the center open spaces of lawn with small groups of beautiful shrubbery. A wide path leads to the little vegetable garden with a few fruit trees, and to the shed at the extreme end of the lot. A narrow path leads by graceful curves to a little flower bed and to a resting place "A," where, if desired, a little pavilion can be erected. The lawn in front of the charming bungalow is open to the street and continuous with those of the adjoining gardens. Two beautiful evergreens are placed on either side of the lawn. Groups of flowering shrubs are planted near the bungalow. On the sides of the dwelling the lot is enclosed by a thin evergreen hedge. There are two little flower beds on either side of the terrace and a larger one extending across the front of the cozy porch. This garden, together with the charming bungalow, can be duplicated in any part of the country, provided proper plants are used to suit the local conditions. For details about the planting list, see pages 8 and 116.

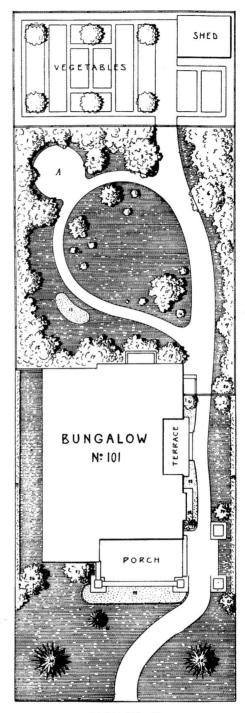

PLAN NO. 19
Size of Lot 50'x150'

NO. 20—ROCK AND WATER GAR-DEN

Picturesque vegetation, blended with rocks and running water, is the most fascinating picture nature can produce. Water is the most important factor in a natural garden. It brings the charm of life and beauty and action into the scenery.

This plan represents an ideal rock and water garden with well-arranged rock-work near the boundary. An imitation spring emerging from a pipe, well hidden in a cleft between rocks, forms a little streamlet, which feeds the charming lily pool. The overflow of the pool, instead of running to waste, is used to feed the adjoining bog garden, which is well stocked with a charming collection of bog plants. The margin of the pool is broken here and there by grassy banks, studded with various plants. The well-constructed rock garden is an imitation of a rocky hillside with crevices and pockets, which provide a home for lovely alpine and many other interesting plants from lower altitudes. Stone walks pass through the little meadow, with a variety of little plants at the sides, which are allowed to crawl into the walk in their natural growth. One of the paths, after crossing the stream-let, ends in a little resting place, hidden from view by a mass of flowering shrubs. An irregular line of beautiful shrubbery is planted along the boundary to hide the fence and the sides of the garage. For details about the planting list, see pages 8 and 116.

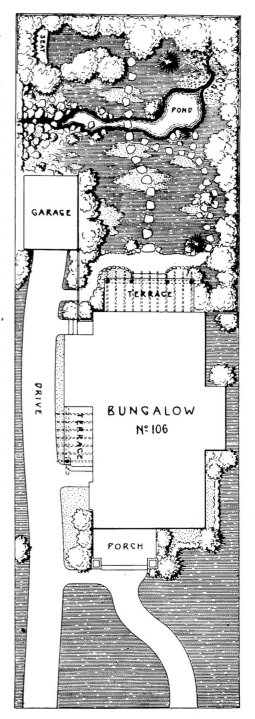

PLAN NO. 20
Size of Lot 50'x150'

NO. 21. ALPINE GARDEN

There is an erroneous idea that the exquisite flowers of alpine regions cannot be grown in gardens of the lowlands. This idea, however, has been dispelled by the fact that most of the lovely alpines have been successfully cultivated in many gardens in the various parts of Europe. The name ''alpine'' is used to denote plants that grow naturally, not only on the high Alps of Switzerland, but on the other high mountain ranges. Alpine plants possess a particular charm when grown in a well-made rock garden amid natural surroundings and isolated from all formal surroundings. This little plan shows a touch of natural scenery with properly arranged rock work. The center of the extreme end forms a miniature cliff adjoining a ravine. A little pool in the center brings the charm of water into the scenery. The winding paths giving access to the different rock beds, are laid out in a natural way —the edges broken and stony and adorned with proper plants. The surface of the alpine garden is covered with plants as far as practical, except a few projecting points. The success and effect of alpine gardens depends entirely on the natural construction of the rock work and the proper arrangement of plants. I will furnish, together with the planting list, little sketches showing the proper construction of rock beds and the right way of planting alpines. Price, $5.00.

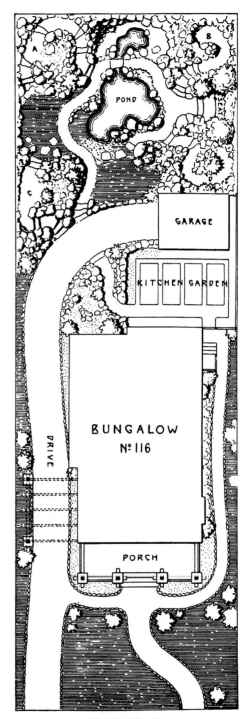

PLAN NO. 21
Size of Lot 50'x150'

NO. 22—OLD ENGLISH GARDEN

This plan shows a charming little English flower garden, entirely surrounded by an evergreen hedge, which gives it the charm of privacy. The garden is laid out in typical formal style with a stone sun-dial in the center of two wide, stone-flagged paths. The long middle path leads from the cozy pergola-covered porch to the extreme end of the garden, where it is terminated by a wooden seat, painted to correspond with the trim of the dwelling. Another similar seat is placed at the end of the other wide path, directly opposite the entrance to the humble kitchen garden. A narrow path follows the outlines of the garden and gives easy access to any of the beds. All the paths are built of old flag stones carefully laid in sand, with small rock plants growing between. The beds are planted with hardy flowers, so selected that throughout the season, there will be a constant succession of bloom, with splendid harmonies of rich and brilliant color. The porch is flanked on either side with beautiful flowering shrubbery, and the pergola is covered with vines, which make the porch a delightful place of rest. From the porch a path branches off and leads to a space between the house and hedge, which is successfully used as a fernery. For details about the planting list, see pages 8 and 116.

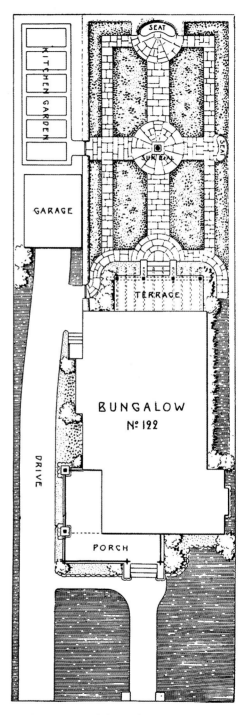

PLAN NO. 22
Size of Lot 50'x150'

NO. 23—OLD ENGLISH GARDEN

Here is another excellent plan for a moderate-sized English flower garden of formal design. A stone sun-dial of simple and inexpensive design marks the intersection of two straight paths, one of which, leading to the garden house, is formed of old flags laid at random, with gravel setting. Flags are also used on the path back of the bungalow and near the entrance gate. All the other paths are either gravel or grass. If grass is used, the side paths leading to the small kitchen gardens, intended for harder use, should be laid in stone. Four flower beds are placed around the stone circle. These are surrounded by a circular path with four angular beds, arranged on its outer edge. Each angular bed being provided with a recess for a garden seat. All the beds are planted with herbaceous plants, so selected that the entire garden will be in gorgeous bloom throughout the season. Flower borders planted mostly with choice flowering shrubs and herbaceous plants, run along the front, the back and the south side of the bungalow. On the front lawn is a group of dwarf evergreens nearer the entrance, and a specimen conifer near the hedge to the left. An evergreen hedge encloses the place on all sides, except the front, which is open to the street. The garage is reached from the alley. For details about the planting list, see pages 8 and 116.

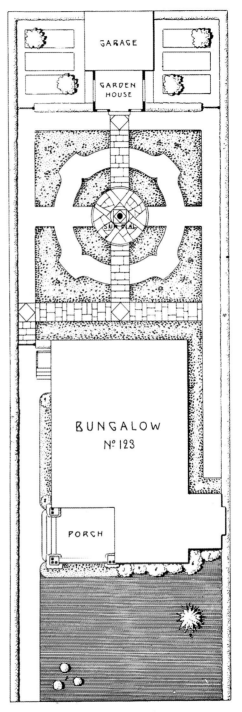

PLAN NO. 23
Size of Lot 50′x150′

NO. 24—FORMAL GARDEN

A very successful combination of a flower garden and orchard is shown on this plan. It is laid out in formal style with a regular-shaped lawn in the center, surrounded by a wide gravel path. A narrow border of pegged-down roses, with a row of standard roses rising from it, follows the outlines of the lawn. A number of fruit trees are planted along the shrubbery hedge, which encloses the garden on all sides. The short narrow path at the far end of the garden leads through a rose arch into the small kitchen garden. A drive, passing under the porte-cochere, runs along the hedge to the garage in the rear of the lot. There are flowering shrubs and herbaceous plants on either side of the kitchen entrance. The lawn in front of the bungalow is open to the street and has a few shrubs and flowers planted near the dwelling and the porch. If an unbroken surface of lawn is desired, the walk leading directly to the front porch can be omitted and the straight line of the remaining narrow path can be broken by groups of shrubbery arranged in front of it. The space between the hedge and the north side of the bungalow offers an ideal place for growing ferns and other plants, which thrive in the shade. For details about the planting list, see pages 8 and 116.

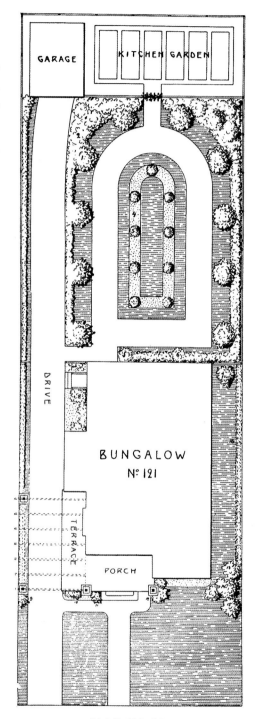

PLAN NO. 24
Size of Lot 50'x150'

NO. 25—ROSE GARDEN

This charming rose garden offers quiet seclusion in its well-planned arrangements. Its commanding feature is the pergola, which covers the terrace and the wide walk along the north boundary of the garden. Beautiful climbing roses and vines cover the pergola almost entirely and make it the pleasantest of out-door resting places. A fence, with a pergola top over-grown with vines and roses, forms the boundary at the extreme end and along the left side of the garden. Shrubbery planted near the terrace and at the far end of the garden, forms a beautiful background for roses. A gravel path encloses a symmetrical lawn, which has a row of standards planted in a narrow border of pegged-down roses. Vines planted near the garage cover its garden side entirely. There are flower borders along the south side of the front porch entrance. A path of stepping stones leads through the fernery along the north side of the bungalow to the garden entrance. The front of the garden is open to the street, being divided by a wide central walk into two lawns, each lawn having a specimen tree (evergreen or palm) in its center and a dwarf evergreen near the entrance. On either side of the bungalow the lot is enclosed by an evergreen hedge. For details about the planting list, see pages 8 and 116.

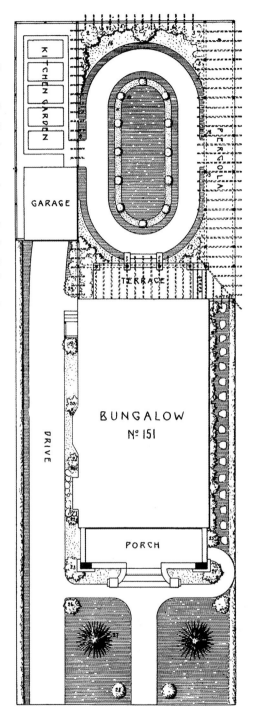

PLAN NO. 25
Size of Lot 50'x150'

NO. 26—ROSE GARDEN

There is a charm about a beautiful rose garden which appeals irresistibly to every lover of flowers. A particularly charming arrangement for a moderate-sized rose garden is shown in this plan. It has four angular beds placed around a circular lawn with a sun-dial in its center and four lovely rose arches covering the short paths leading to it. A beautiful semi-circular arbor, placed in the middle of the rose bed at the extreme end of the garden, provides a delightful place of rest, where the eye encounters a charming picture in every direction and where the fragrance of roses is inhaled with every breath. There is one garden seat in the shrubbery border back of the bungalow and two other ones opposite each other, in the borders along the hedge. All walks are planned in turf, but the one to the left, leading to the kitchen garden and intended for harder use, should be laid with stepping stones. An evergreen hedge encloses the place on all sides, giving it the charm of seclusion. The planting in front of the bungalow is simple and pleasant. There are two dwarf evergreens on either side of the entrance, three tall conifers and beautiful shrubs planted in groups along the walks and near the house. A path of stepping stones leads to the perennial border running along the hedge on the right side of the building. For details about the planting list, see pages 8 and 116.

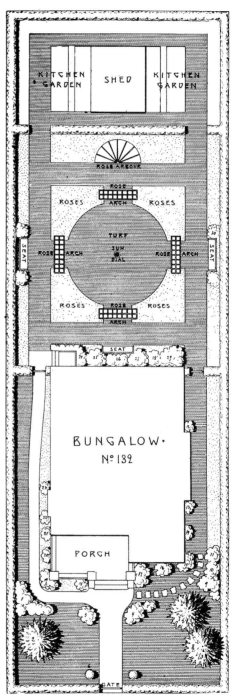

PLAN NO. 26
Size of Lot 50′x150′

NO. 27—ROSE GARDEN

Here is another beautiful rose garden laid out on formal lines somewhat similar to the preceding one. It has four angular beds, arranged around a square lawn, in the middle of which stands a bird bath. Double arches luxuriantly overgrown with climbing roses mark the intersections of the four grass walks, which surround the angular beds. Two garden seats are placed opposite each other in the flower borders, which run along the hedge on either side of the garden, and a third one in the shrubbery back of the bungalow. A curved seat, with a sun-dial in front of it, is seen in the rose border at the extreme end of the garden. Passing through the rose arches the two lateral walks lead to the kitchen garden in the rear of the lot. An evergreen hedge completely encircles the place and gives it a delightful feeling of privacy. The front yard shows a very effective planting scheme. There are three specimen shade trees set near the hedge and groups of beautiful flowering shrubs planted on either side of the walk and near the bungalow. A path of stepping stones, passing through groups of shrubbery, leads to the wide grass walk, bordered by herbaceous plants and ferns. From this point, looking through the rose arches, a fine long vista is obtained. A narrow walk to the left leads to the kitchen. For details about the planting list, see pages 8 and 116.

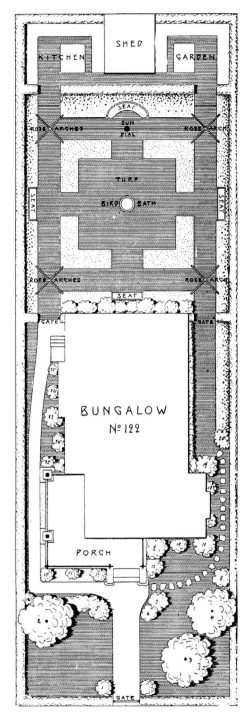

PLAN NO. 27
Size of Lot 50'x150'

NO. 28—FORMAL GARDEN

An unusual and very interesting feature of this beautiful formal garden is the circular pergola which forms the central motive in the distance. It is luxuriantly overgrown with climbing roses and vines of beautiful flowers succeeding each other so closely that scarcely a month passes without the fragrant bloom. In the foreground is a circular path, surrounding a grass plot with a flower bed in the center and a narrow border along its edge. It is connected with the pergola by a short walk, flanked on either side by a dwarf evergreen. Beautiful flowering shrubs densely planted in effective groups along the boundary of the garden, render the place more secluded and private. On the left side of the garden, entirely screened by shrubbery, is the garage and a small vegetable garden with a path of stepping stones leading to it from the pergola. The planting in the front yard is simple and most effective. It consists of beautiful shrubs planted in groups on either side of the curved walk and along the boundary to the right. Shrubs and herbaceous plants are used in the border along the drive and in front of the bungalow. A tall specimen evergreen is shown on the lawn near the drive and two dwarf ones complete the group flanking the entrance. For details about the planting list, see pages 8 and 116.

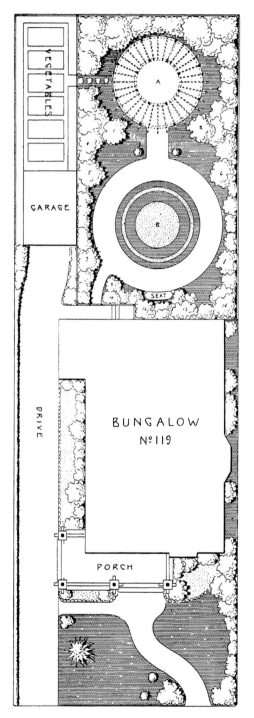

PLAN NO. 28
Size of Lot 50′x150′

CALIFORNIA GARDENS

NO. 29—NATURAL GARDEN

This plan shows a charming small garden laid out in French landscape style. It has a curved walk, which encircles an irregular-shaped lawn, planted along its edge with effective groups of evergreens and shrubs. In the corner to the right, enclosed by a dense mass of shrubbery, is a semi-circular space for garden seats and table. The pergola-covered porch in front of the breakfast room is flanked by groups of choice shrubs and overgrown with vines; on the lawn in front of it is a round flower bed, with a dwarf evergreen on either side. Dense masses of various shrubs enclose the garden on all sides, giving it the charm of privacy. A small piece of ground is set apart for fruit trees and vegetables in the background beside the garage. The front is open to the street, the lawn being divided by the wide walk into two sections, each having a specimen evergreen in its center and a dwarf one near the entrance. Beautiful shrubs and herbaceous plants are planted in front of the porch and along the sides of the bungalow. The drive to the left, running along the boundary formed by a narrow flower border, enters the back yard through a gate, which shuts off the view from the street. Omitting the driveway and garage this plan could be used on a 40-foot lot. For details about the planting list, see pages 8 and 116.

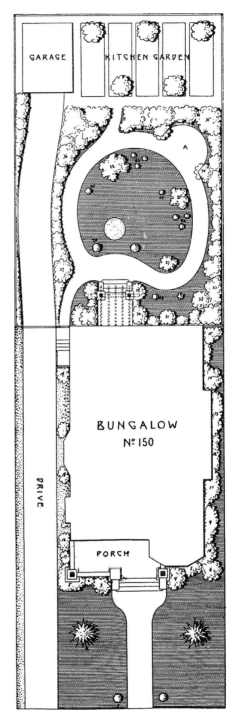

PLAN NO. 29
Size of Lot 50′x150′

89

NO. 30—SEMI-FORMAL GARDEN

A most successful use of the pergola is made in this plan by running it across the entire end of the garden, forming a boundary and screen for the kitchen garden beyond. On the left, the pergola is widened to form an out-door living room, which, with its garden seats and table, presents a delightful place to rest and forget one's cares amid charming surroundings. The feature in the foreground of the garden is a round lily pool, surrounded by a margin of various plants growing on the waterside. The presence of water in the garden adds that touch of life to the scene, which portrays nature in vivid reflections from the surface of the pool. A path, on the axial line of the pool, flanked on either side by a row of standard roses, connects the circular path with the pergola. Another narrow path turns to the left, back of the garage, and passing under a shade tree, leads to the pergola-covered resting place. The planting is composed chiefly of flowering shrubs, arranged in attractive groups in front of the pergola, along the boundary and on the sides of the building. A drive, passing under a porte-cochere, leads to the garage, overgrown with beautiful vines. Herbaceous plants and shrubs are planted along the drive near the bungalow and around the front porch. On the sides, the place is bordered by an evergreen hedge. The kitchen garden, in the back part of the lot, contains eight fruit trees, besides a few vegetables. For details about the planting list, see pages 8 and 116.

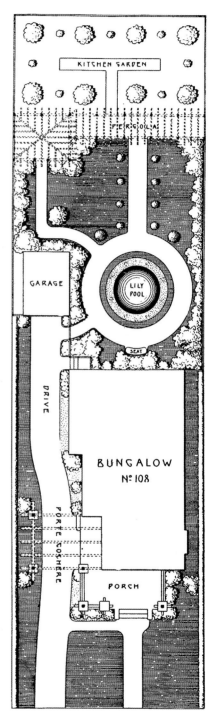

PLAN NO. 30
Size of Lot 50'x175'

90

NO. 31—FORMAL GARDEN

An excellent plan, designed for a corner lot and suitable also for a 50-foot inside lot. It shows a circular path, enclosing a round lawn with a flower bed of herbaceous plants in the center and four narrow borders of low shrubs, alternated with four single plants, along its edge. A pergola-covered terrace, overgrown with vines and flanked on either side by beautiful flowering shrubs forms the foreground of the garden. Two curved paths, passing through the shrubbery, lead to the entrance gates. The background is planted with masses of shrubbery, which screens the garage and the small vegetable garden. In each upper corner is a recess A in which comfortable garden seats can be placed. Shrubs form the boundary on one side of the garden, the opposite side being left open to give the passers-by a glimpse of the scenery within. There are two specimens of coniferous trees and a few dwarf evergreens on the front lawn. Choice shrubs are planted along the boundary on the sides of the bungalow and in front of the porch. The kitchen entrance and the short walk, which leads from the side street to the garden gate, are screened with groups of shrubs. The garage in the rear of the lot is entered from the side street. For details about the planting list, see pages 8 and 116.

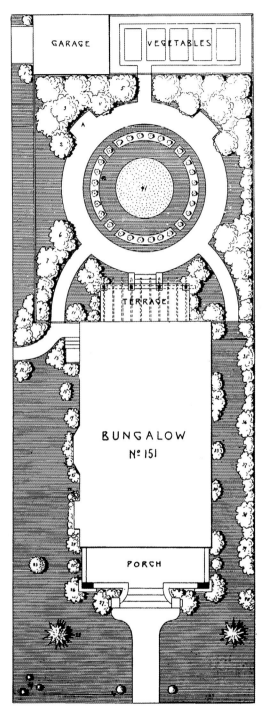

PLAN NO. 31
Size of Corner Lot 55′x150′

NO. 32—NATURAL GARDEN

This plan shows how a small garden, of simple design, may be given character by its contents. It is laid out in French landscape style with curved paths enclosing an egg-shaped lawn, planted with effective groups of shrubs and evergreens. A cozy pergola-covered terrace, overgrown with vines and screened on the sides by shrubbery, occupies the near end of the garden. On the lawn, opposite the terrace, is a round flower bed, flanked on either side by dwarf trees. Dense masses of shrubbery enclose the garden on all sides, giving it the delightful feeling of privacy. An octagonal pavilion, surrounded by shrubbery, is shown in the upper corner to the left, and a semi-circular recess for a garden seat occupies the corner to the right. The planting on the lawn in front of the bungalow consists of specimens of coniferous trees and dwarf evergreens, arranged in attractive groupings. Herbaceous plants and shrubs are planted around the porch, along the sides of the bungalow and near the kitchen entrance. The entrance to the garage is from the side street. This plan is suitable for a corner or a 50-foot inside lot. For details about the planting list, see pages 8 and 116.

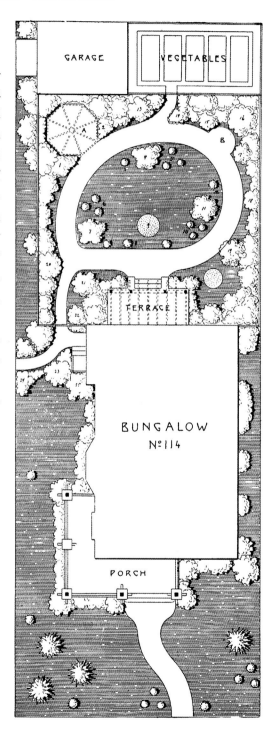

PLAN NO. 32
Size of Corner Lot 55'x150'

NO. 33—ROCK AND WATER GAR-DEN

Fortunate is the owner who has a garden which is beautified by the presence of water. It will greatly enhance the charm of his garden and make it more interesting and picturesque. An ideal garden, containing water in its various forms, is shown on this plan, designed for a corner lot. The center of the garden is occupied by a pond, where choice water lilies and other aquatics are grown. The overflow of the pond supplies the necessary water for the adjoining bog garden in which plants requiring an extra degree of moisture are grown. The garage in the background is almost hidden by natural grouping of tall plants. A little artificial streamlet, emerging from a pipe, completely hidden in a cleft of the rockwork near the fence, gives actual life to the scene as it splashes over rocks and boulders. A narrow walk, as informal as possible, with broken and stony edges, crosses the streamlet over a rustic bridge and ends in a little vegetable garden, well hidden by a group of trees and shrubs. From the second bridge a little path of stepping stones gives access to the pond from the street side. For details about the planting list, see pages 8 and 116.

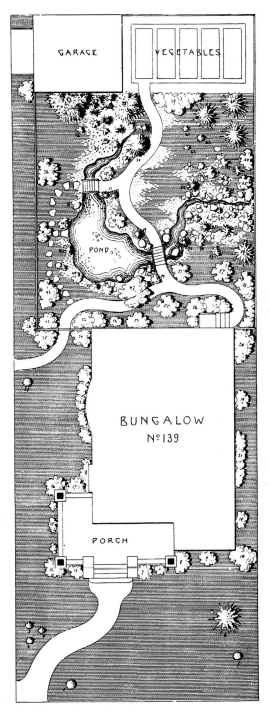

PLAN NO. 33
Size of Corner Lot 55'x150'

NO. 34—NATURAL GARDEN

Here is a good example of a garden treated in landscape style. It is open to the side street and has a winding path leading from the side porch to a circular resting place in the back part of the garden. Beautiful shrubs surround the garden from three sides, the fourth one being left open, presenting a good vista from the side street. Groups of shrubs, cleverly arranged on either side of the path leading to the side porch and the kitchen entrance, hide the latter entirely. Two specimens of tall coniferous trees and several groups of smaller ones, together with a few choice shrubs, complete the effective planting scheme on the back lawn. The front lawn being treated similarly, has a few shrubs and a beautiful coniferous tree near the boundary to the left. A wide approach, entering the place from the corner between effective groupings of shrubs and dwarf evergreens, leads in elegant curves to the front porch. For details about the planting list, see pages 8 and 116.

PLAN NO. 34
Size of Corner Lot 60'x135'

NO. 35—FORMAL GARDEN

An exceptionally good design for a small formal garden suited to a corner or a 50-foot inside lot. The central feature of it is a lily pool, surrounded by a wide margin of beautiful water loving plants. A wide path, running across the place with a central walk and two lateral ones converging towards the center of the pool, form two irregular pentagons, each one having a tall evergreen in the center and five beautiful flowering herbaceous plants surrounding it. There are two large, comfortable seats placed in the shrubbery forming the background of the garden, and a smaller one near the bungalow on the axial line of the garden. The planting in the front yard consists mostly of choice shrubs, arranged in attractive groupings, along the sides of the bungalow near the porches and in front of the kitchen entrance, hiding the latter entirely from the street. There are two specimens of tall evergreens and three dwarf ones on the front lawn, as shown on the plan. The small garden in the back yard contains a few vegetable beds. For details about the planting list, see pages 8 and 116.

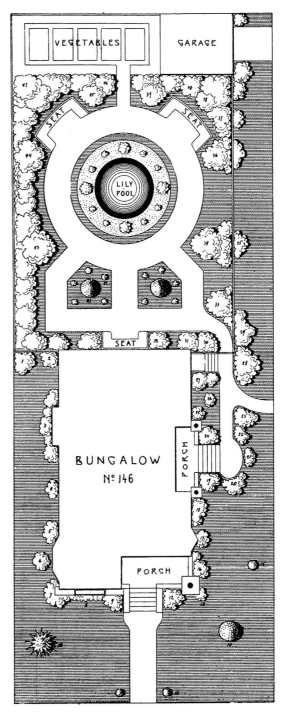

PLAN NO. 35
Size of Corner Lot 60'x150'

NO. 36—NATURAL GARDEN

It is difficult to describe the beauty of this garden. The plant-scheme—silver gray and blue. The best blue flowering perennials, planted in natural groups, against a background of glaucous-leaved shrubs and silver gray evergreens. makes a planting magnificent for effectiveness, and at the same time preserves the restfulness and charm of Nature. This free planting does not disturb the quiet turf and grassy walks winding between the beautiful flower groups. The different flowers used in this garden are so selected that, throughout the season, there will be a constant succession of bloom. The planting in the front yard is carried out with a similar effect. The four silver gray coniferous trees on the lawn form effective groups with shrubs of mostly glaucous foliage. A path of stepping stones, passing between the different groups of shrubbery, leads to the back garden from the right side of the bunga-low. An evergreen hedge encloses the place on all sides. For details about the planting list, see pages 8 and 116.

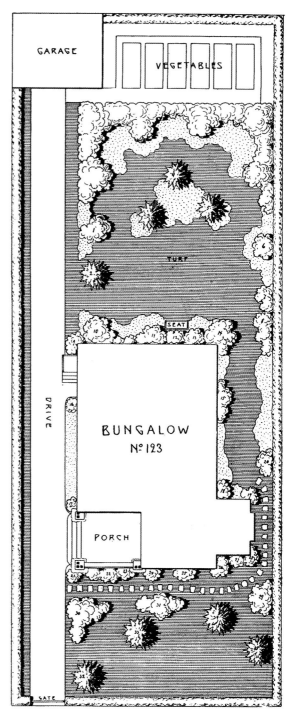

PLAN NO. 36
Size of Lot 60'x150'

NO. 37—IRIS GARDEN

The Irises are amongst the loveliest and most effective of flowers which have been specialized in gardens. Nothing can excel them in charm, and the delicate grace of their orchid-like blooms impresses every lover of beauty. There are many charming varieties which, as they flower, give opportunities for successive color groups. The Iris is easy to cultivate and thrives abundantly in any good garden soil and increases in beauty from year to year. They bloom luxuriantly and the different species embrace a flowering season, which reaches from the early spring until late in July. This plan shows a garden, in which many varieties of Iris are grown in natural groupings; the little shallow pond in the center is devoted to those requiring moisture to develop their magnificent blooms. Paths of stepping

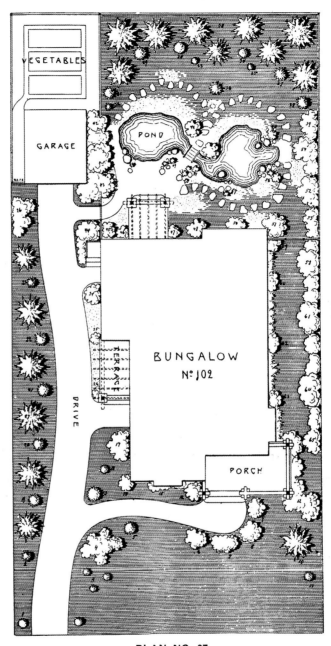

PLAN NO. 37
Size of Lot 70'x135'

stones wind around the pond and give easy access to the various groups of Iris. The background is planted with evergreens and the sides with flowering shrubs. For details about the planting list, see pages 8 and 116.

NO. 38—FORMAL GARDEN

This is a very convenient arrangement for a garden in which flowers, fruit trees and vegetables are combined in one. A semi-circular lawn, with a flower bed in its center and a few herbaceous plants along the edge, forms the main feature in the foreground of the garden. A wide central path, bounded on either side by fruit trees, leads from the semi-circle to the far end of the garden, ending in a resting place, entirely surrounded by shrubbery. The space beyond the fruit trees contains the vegetable garden, screened on three sides by a hedge of fruit shrubs. A hedge of beautiful flowering shrubs forms the boundary on either side of the bungalow. The front has a semi-circular drive enclosing a lawn, with a round flower bed opposite the porch entrance and eight dwarf evergreens arranged in symmetrical groups. A tall specimen of a coniferous tree, groups of ornamental shrubs and herbaceous plants complete the symmetrical planting scheme on either side of the bungalow. The garage is entered from the alley in the rear of the lot. For details about the planting list see pages 8 and 116.

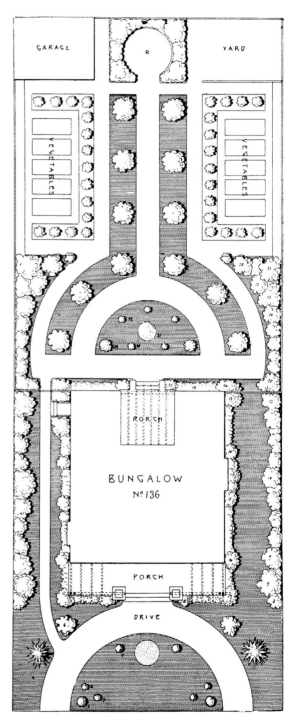

PLAN NO. 38
Size of Lot 70′x175′

NO. 39—JAPANESE TEA
GARDEN (Cha-niva)

This plan, designed for a
corner lot, illustrates a charming Japanese Tea Garden in
which the lovely Iris plays a
prominent part. It contains a
shallow pool, crossed by two
rustic b r i d g e s of single
planks, where many varieties
of Iris develop their exquisite
blossoms, flashing in the sun-
light with prismatic hues of
gem-like splendor. A pergola
porch covered with the glorious wistaria a d d s to t h e
beauty and coziness of the
garden. From the porch, a
walk of stepping stones leads
to the entrance gates and another to the little tea room in
a remote corner of the garden. Stone lanterns ''L'', a
stone well ''W'', s c r e e n s
''S'', groups of rocks—including t h e indispensable
''Guardian Stone'' — many
trees and shrubs complete the
ornamental features of the
ground. The low garden
shrubs, which are used between rocks and stone lanterns upon hillsides, are usually clipped into hemispher-

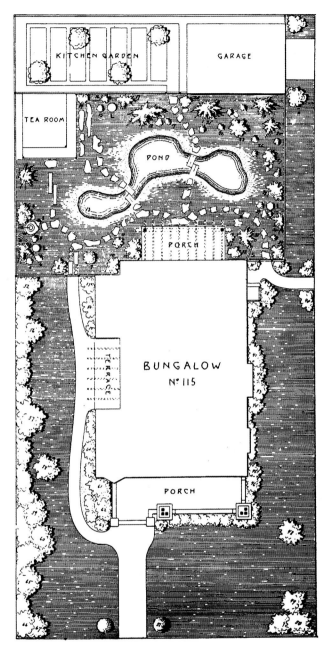

PLAN NO. 39
Size of Corner Lot 75'x150'

ical forms representing round masses of different shades of green and known
under the native term ''Marumono'' or round material. For details about
the planting list, see pages 8 and 116.

NO. 40—FORMAL GARDEN

Here is a wonderfully beautiful garden of an unusual design. It has a circular pergola, enclosing a lawn w i t h a lily-pond placed in its center and box-bordered beds, planted with brilliantly flowering perennials, arranged in front of it. Beautiful roses and vines cover the pergola entirely, making it a fragrant and pleasant retreat on hot summer days. A thick evergreen hedge, at least five feet high, encloses the garden on three sides, giving it shelter and privacy. A drive enters the grounds from the front at the left-hand corner, and passing u n d e r a porte-cochere, leads to the garage in the enclosed service yard. The space beyond the garage is reserved for five fruit trees and a few vegetables. The planting in

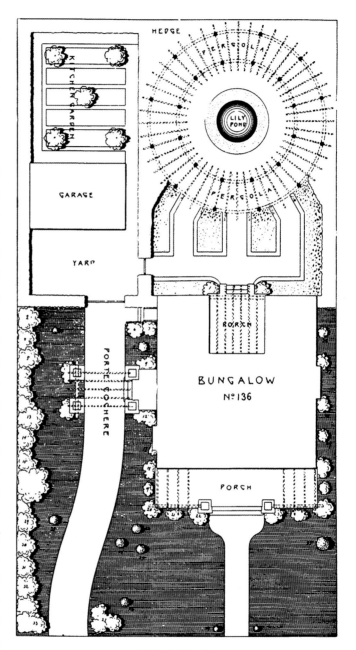

PLAN NO. 40
Size of Lot 80′x150′

the front consists of several choice evergreens and groups of shrubs along the boundary and near the sides of the bungalow. For details about the planting list, see pages 8 and 116.

NO. 41—COLONIAL GARDEN

Here is a typical design, which was often used in the colonies—North and South. It is a great wheel in which the central fountain takes the place of the hub. The radiating paths represent the spokes, which mark off the box-bordered flower beds, and a circular path encloses the whole like a tire. Each flower bed is planted with dwarf evergreens and beautiful perennials. A wide path, bounded by tall evergreens, runs across the garden front of the house, with three other paths connecting it with the center. Each of the diagonal paths, after crossing the circular one, lead to a resting place in the upper corners of the garden. A thick evergreen hedge encloses the place on all sides. The planting in the front yard consists of four beautiful evergreens, a few shade trees and many choice shrubs arranged in effective groupings on the lawn. For details about the planting list, see pages 8 and 116.

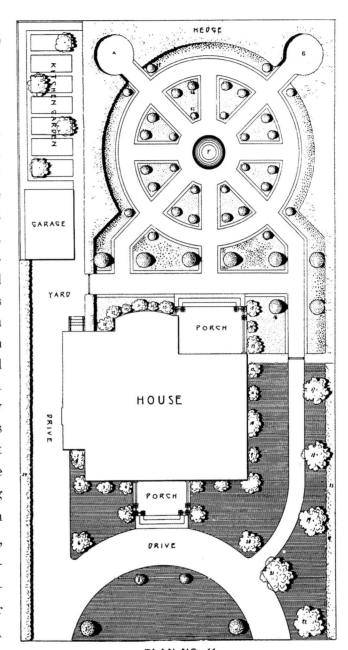

PLAN NO. 41
Size of Lot 80'x150'

CALIFORNIA GARDENS

NO. 42—COLONIAL GARDEN

The Colonial or Old-fashioned Gardens were laid out after the Italian method with box bordered flower beds (slightly modified by the influence of English, Dutch or French colonists). The centers of these gardens are usually formed by a fountain, a sun-dial or bushy box wood specimen. This plan represents a good example of an old-fashioned garden with a group of evergreens in the central circle. The radiating paths divide the box-bordered flower parterres, each parterre having an evergreen in its center—forms an outer circle. One evergreen is placed in each of the small corner beds opposite the diagonal paths. A box-lined flower bed runs along the thick evergreen hedge, which encloses the place on three sides. The planting in front and on the sides of the house is very attractive. It consists of two beautiful shade trees and many evergreens and shrubs arranged in effective groups on the lawn, as shown on the plan. A drive, running along the hedge, leads to the garage in the enclosed service yard. The space beyond the garage contains three fruit trees and a few vegetable beds. For details about the planting list, see pages 8 and 116.

NO. 43—SEMI-FORMAL GARDEN

The plan on the following page shows a very successful treatment of the grounds in a semi-formal way. The back garden has a regular-shaped lawn with standard roses, alternated with low evergreens planted along the edge. Two round flower beds are shown in the central portion, which is sunk below the level of the path. A row of beautiful flowering trees line the outer edge of the path and a hedge of choice shrubs encloses the entire place. From the semi-formal part of the enclosed garden one passes into the front yard, which is carried out in excellent landscape style. Beautiful shrubs, planted in irregular groups along the boundary, form a splendid background for the different evergreens, arranged in effective groupings, on the lawn on either side of the bungalow. The lawn in front has two low evergreens flanking the approach. One specimen of a tall coniferous tree with three smaller ones near the left boundary and a few shrubs and evergreens form a group along the drive, which enters the grounds at the corner to the right and passing under the porte-cochere makes a spacious turn in front of the garage. For details about the planting list see page 116.

CALIFORNIA GARDENS

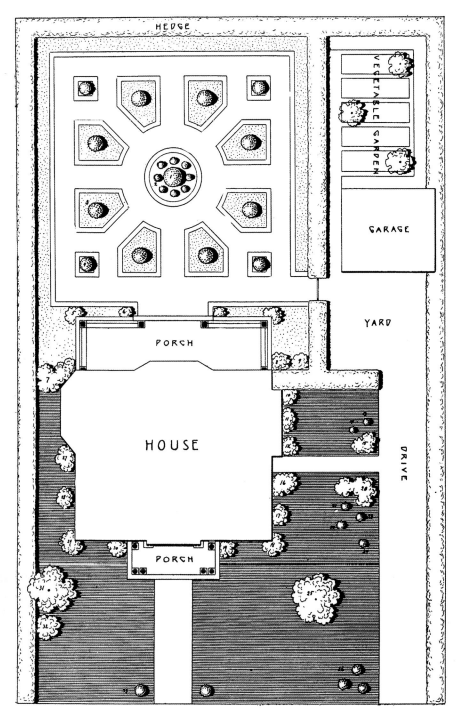

PLAN NO. 42
Size of Lot 90'x140'

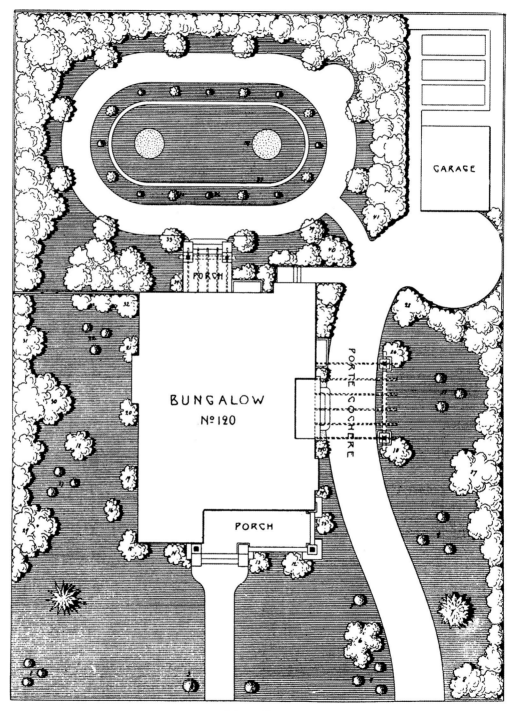

GARAGE

PORCH

BUNGALOW
Nº 120

PORTE COCHERE

PORCH

PLAN NO. 43
Size of Lot 100'x135'

CALIFORNIA GARDENS

NO. 44—FORMAL GARDEN

The plan on page 106 shows a garden laid out in formal style and containing many attractive features. The back garden has a regular-shaped lawn with a flower-bed and fountain placed on its axial line—tall evergreens and standard roses being planted along the edge. Opposite the fountain at the far end of the garden is a comfortable seat. The background and sides are formed by a dense hedge clipped into shape, with standard thorns connected by garlands of beautiful flowering vines placed along its front. There is a cozy resting place enclosed by shrubbery near the boundary to the right. At this point a narrow path passing through the shrubbery leads to a small rose garden on the south side of the bungalow. It has three circular rose beds placed on the central line of the elongated lawn and surrounded by eight standard roses connected with garlands of charming vines. Ornamental trees and shrubs line the drive to the garage and four low evergreens, rising from a narrow flower border, form the planting on the lawn in front of the entrance. A thick hedge protects and screens the place from either side. For details about the planting list see pages 8 and 116.

NO. 45—FORMAL AND LANDSCAPE GARDEN

The plan on page 107 is for a garden in which the back is laid out on strictly formal lines, while the front yard is treated in landscape style. The rectangular lawn with rounded projections in the middle of each side forms a pleasing geometrical design. It has standard roses planted in the narrow flower border along its edge. Four specimens of tall evergreens are placed in each corner and four circular beds form the center of the rounded sections. Beautiful ornamental trees line the path on the outer edge and a thick hedge encloses the whole place. A small pergola, covering a stone table and two seats, is shown near the garage. The drive enters the grounds from the front near the right-hand corner and passing under the porte-cochere leads to the garage in the service yard. The planting in the front yard is very attractive. There are three tall conifers forming an effective group near the boundary to the left and one dwarf evergreen is placed on each side of the entrance. Two shade trees are planted near the drive and a group of shrubs and evergreens flank its entrance on the left-hand side. A thick hedge of shrubs screens the place from the sides. For details about the planting list see pages 8 and 116.

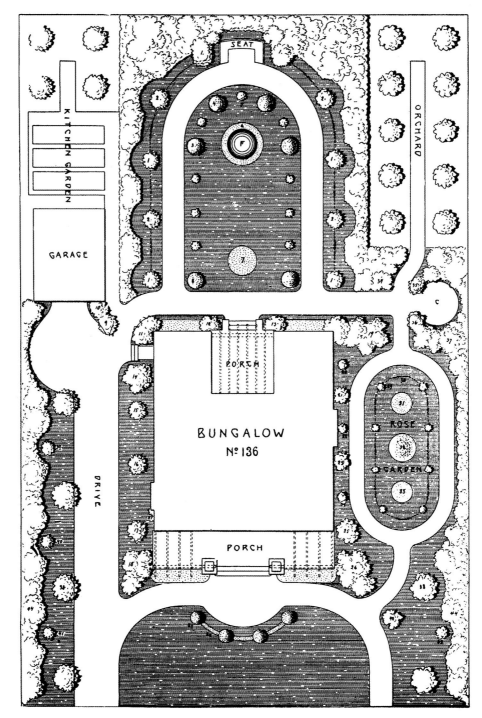

PLAN NO. 44
Size of Lot 100'x150'

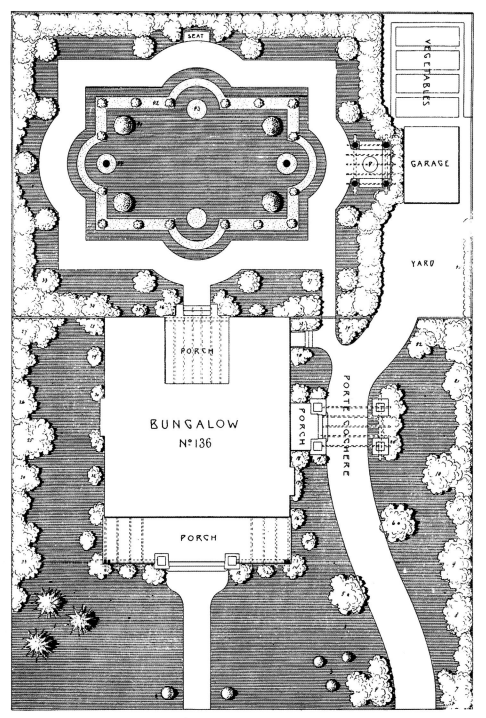

VEGETABLES

GARAGE

YARD

SEAT

PORCH

BUNGALOW
Nº 136

PORCH

PORCH

PORTE COCHERE

PORCH

PLAN NO. 45
Size of Lot 100'x150'

NO. 46—FORMAL GARDEN

An excellent design for a formal garden is shown in this plan. The center of the garden is formed by a charming lily pool surrounded by four choice evergreens and four angular box-bordered beds planted with evergreens and flowers. A semi-circular seat with an ornamental tree on either side and a sun-dial in the center occupies the far end of the garden. There are two small pergolas, with stone seats placed between the pillars and a table in the center, which add much to the beauty and coziness of the garden. A wide perennial bor-

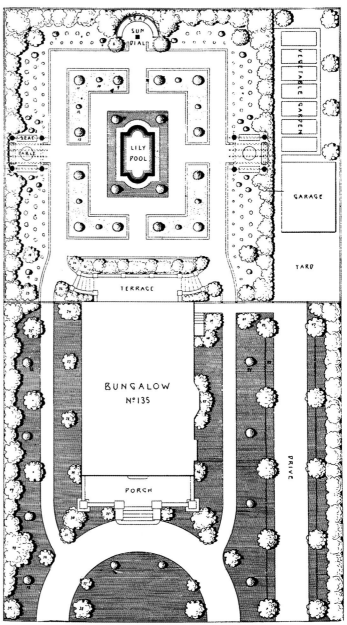

PLAN NO. 46
Size of Lot 100'x175'

der bounded by a thick hedge runs around the three sides of the place. The drive is lined on either side by five ornamental trees connected with garlands of beautiful vines. For details about the planting list see pages 8 and 116.

NO. 47—SEMI-FORMAL
AND LANDSCAPE
GARDEN

This plan shows a good example of a garden treated
semi-formally. It has a circular lawn with evergreens and
standard roses planted along
the circumference and a formal
fountain placed in the center,
surrounded by a margin of
plants. A pergola occupies
the back-ground of the garden.
The irregular-shaped lawn at
the near end of the garden is
treated in French landscape
style with trees and shrubs
arranged in attractive groups
marking the junctions of paths.
A hedge of shrubs forms the
boundary on both sides, the
one on the right-hand side
serving as a screen to the garage and kitchen garden beyond. The planting on the
side of the house in front of
the porte-cochere is carried out

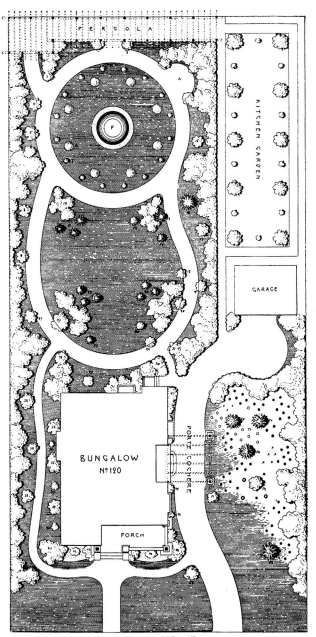

PLAN NO. 47
Size of Lot 100'x200'

in an effective color scheme—silver gray and blue—with blue flowering perennials planted between groups of trees and shrubs of glaucous foliage. For
details about the planting list, see pages 8 and 116.

CALIFORNIA GARDENS

NO. 48—FORMAL AND LANDSCAPE GARDEN

The diagram on the opposite page shows a small suburban estate with pretty gardens, orchard, tennis-court, green-house and garage—all the conveniences of a modern country home. A formal garden of simple and pleasing design occupies the space beyond the house. The central path with the lily-pond in the middle, a semi-circular seat and a sun-dial at the far end are placed on the axial line of the library window, dividing the garden into two lawns, each lawn having two evergreens and four angular flower beds. A thick evergreen hedge surrounds the garden on all sides and five evergreens placed in back of the semi-circular hedge form a splendid background for the seat. Passing through the arched openings of the hedge to the left, one enters an enclosed tennis-court. It is terminated by a pergola, occupying the whole width and separating it from a small garden beyond. A large shade tree, having a circular seat around its base, occupies the center of this garden, and a beautiful herbaceous border runs along the hedge. The space in front of the house is laid out in natural or landscape style with trees and shrubs arranged in attractive groups. For details about the planting list see pages 8 and 116.

NO. 49—FORMAL AND LANDSCAPE GARDEN

On page 112 is the plan for another well-ordered and complete suburban estate. The grounds in front of the residence are laid out in natural or landscape style with trees and shrubs planted in irregular groups along the sides, near the drive and paths, creating a beautiful scenery. A narrow path leads into the enclosed formal garden, where four angular flower-beds placed around a lily-pond form a simple design. The middle path extends to the right and passing under a beautiful vine-covered pergola leads to a summer house. Back of the residence is a long pergola, bounded on the right-hand side with a wide perennial border and terminated by an octagonal arbor. Running parallel with the pergola are a series of rose arches, connected by side-pieces and forming a charming division between the flower garden and tennis-lawn. In the middle of the path which connects both arbors, and just opposite the small summer house, is a sun-dial with eight low evergreens planted around it. From the arbor to the left is a wide grass walk terminated by a semi-circular seat and lined on either side with a beautiful perennial border. For details about the planting list see pages 8 and 116.

CALIFORNIA GARDENS

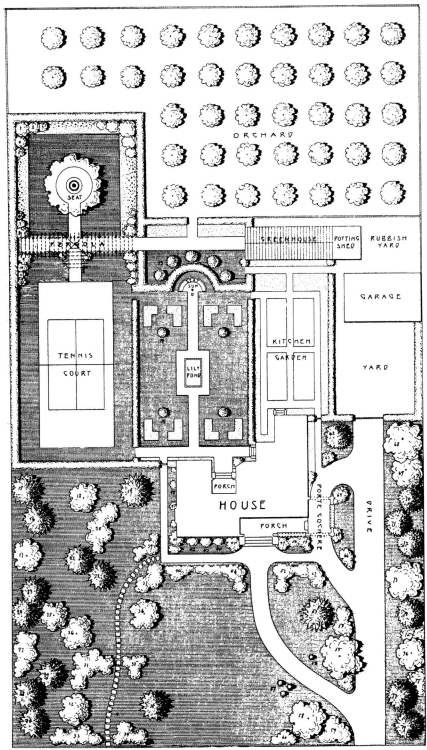

PLAN NO. 48
Size of Lot 200'x350'

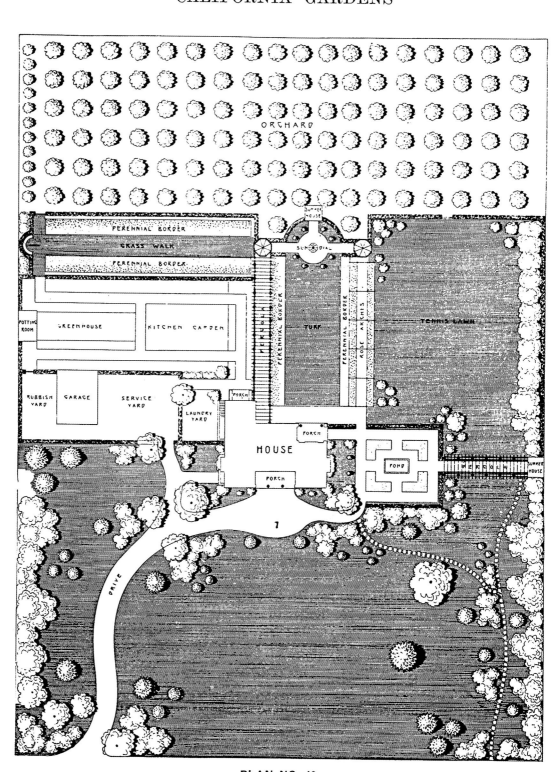

PLAN NO. 49
Size of Lot 300'x400'

CALIFORNIA GARDENS

NO. 50—LANDSCAPE AND FORMAL GARDEN

The plan on the following page represents an ideal country estate provided with all the luxuries answering the demands of modern life. It is located on the corner of two intersecting streets and covers about ten acres. The house is set back 300 feet from the street and has a long southern front facing the beautiful landscape, in which the lake forms the main feature. A long winding drive enters the grounds from the right-hand corner and after passing through groups of beautiful shrubs and trees makes a turn to the left and reaches the garden forecourt in front of the terrace, from which point many charming vistas are obtained. Proceeding to the left the drive crosses a small rustic bridge and winding its way through the beautiful landscape leads to the exit in the left-hand corner of the grounds. There are many paths which, passing through the landscape, lead to the points of interest and create fine vistas. Opposite the little lily-pond on the left-hand side of the path the color scheme of the landscape is silver gray and blue—varieties of blue flowering perennials being planted against a background of glaucous leaved shrubs and trees. Other special color schemes—white and red, yellow and white, yellow and red, dark blue and autumn tints—are carried out in the shrubbery, which forms the screen to the orchard from the south side. After passing this beautiful scenery we enter the charming heath garden, where great masses of heath of harmonious colorings are grouped together, creating a most effective picture. Near the hedge, just opposite the entrance to the formal garden, is a beautiful shade-tree with a circular seat at its base. From this point we get beautiful vistas whichever way we look. Back of the residence is the formal garden. It is completely surrounded by a beautiful pergola and consists of four flower beds placed around a sun-dial, which marks the intersection of two wide central paths.

To the right and left from this formal garden and only separated by a pergola are two charming rose gardens. There are many varieties of roses and a series of rose arches placed over the central path, which leads to the long and wide grass walk flanked on either side by beautiful perennial borders. At the far end of this walk is a simi-circular seat with a shade-tree in front of it. The space between the two flower-bordered grass walks is reserved for a tennis-lawn. The rest is explained on the plan and needs no further comment. For details about the planting list see pages 8 and 116.

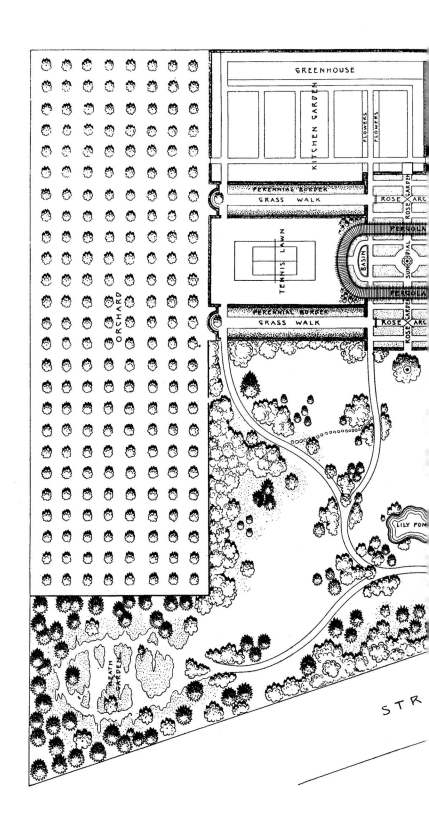

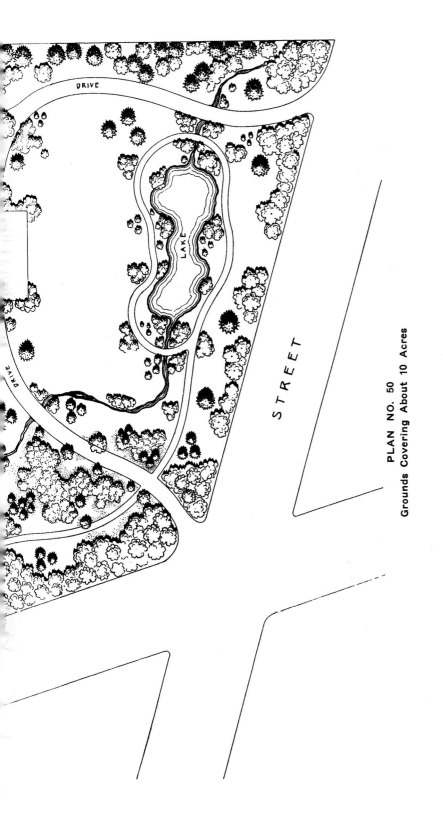

DRIVE

DRIVE

DRIVE

LAKE

STREET

PLAN NO. 50
Grounds Covering About 10 Acres

More Schiffer Titles

www.schifferbooks.com

The Art of Garden Design in Italy. H. Inigo Triggs. Study great gardens in Rome, Florence, Milan, and visit the Vatican, royal palaces, and secluded cloisters at the turn of the century with one of Britain's most important architects. Inspiration for anyone planning an estate garden and an indespensible reference for historians.
Size: 9" x 12" • 156 b/w photos & 94 line drawings • 272 pp. • ISBN: 978-0-7643-2666-0 • hard cover • $49.95

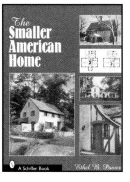

The Smaller American House. Ethel B. Power. This books presents work by some of the e arly 20th century's most notable architects, including Dwight James Baum, Wallace Frost, John F. Staub, Wallace Neff, George Washington Smith, Eleanor Raymond and Henry Atherton Frost. The house styles include Classic Colonial, Spanish Revival, Creole, and Storybook Style. Each homes includes a floor plan.
Size: 8 1/2" x 11" • 130 b/w photos & 105 line drawings • 100 pp. • ISBN: 978-0-7643-2769-8 • soft cover • $19.95

Homes in a Box: Modern Homes from Sears Roebuck. A facsimile reproduction of the Sears Modern Homes catalog. Over a hundred home kits were offered by Sears Roebuck in the early 1900s, either as simple kits with only the blueprints and bill-of-materials or as complete homes with all materials and finishes. Among the architects who contributed designs was Frank Lloyd Wright, and several homes reflect the Arts & Crafts movement. Thousands of these homes are still standing and are beginning to be recognized as architectural treasures.
Size: 10 1/2" x 8 1/2" • 129 photos •120 pp. ISBN: 0-7643-0432-1 •soft cover • $19.95

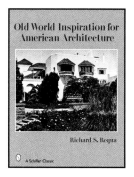

Old World Inspiration for American Architecture. *New Edition.* Richard S. Requa, A.I.A.. This classic resource for authentic Mediterranean and Spanish architecture was compiled in 1929 by the pioneer architect of its revival style. Its 144 plates display many country and city dwellings, interiors, exteriors, and architectural, garden, and ironwork details.
Size: 9" x 12" • 144 b/w photos • 344 pp. • ISBN: 978-0-7643-2668-4 • hard cover • $59.95

Schiffer books may be ordered from your local bookstore, or they may be ordered directly from the publisher by writing to:

Schiffer Publishing, Ltd.
4880 Lower Valley Rd
Atglen PA 19310
(610) 593-1777; Fax (610) 593-2002
E-mail: Info@schifferbooks.com

Please visit our web site catalog at www.schifferbooks.com or write for a free catalog. Please include $3.95 for shipping and handling for the first two books and $1.00 for each additional book. Free shipping for orders of $100 or more.

Printed in China